❋ THE PONY EXPRESS ❋
A Photographic History

Bill and Jan Moeller

MOUNTAIN PRESS PUBLISHING COMPANY
Missoula, Montana
2002

Cover Image: Pony Express Monument
by Herman MacNeil, St. Joseph, Missouri

Library of Congress Cataloging-in-Publication Data

Moeller, Bill, 1930-
   The Pony Express : a photographic history / Bill and Jan Moeller.
      p. cm.
Includes bibliographical references and index.
  ISBN 0-87842-470-9 (pbk. : alk. paper)
 1. Pony express—History—Pictorial works. 2. Postal service—United
States—History—Pictorial works. 3. Stagecoach stations—West
(U.S.)—History—Pictorial works. I. Moeller, Jan, 1930- II. Title.
  HE6375.P65 M63 2003
  383'.143'0973—dc21

2002154001

PRINTED IN HONG KONG BY MANTEC PRODUCTION COMPANY

Mountain Press Publishing Company
P.O. Box 2399 • Missoula, MT 59806
406-728-1900

❋ DEDICATION ❋

For Joe and Vicki,
our favorite trail companions,
with affection

❊ CONTENTS ❊

❈ ACKNOWLEDGMENTS ❈

WE OWE OUR THANKS TO MANY PEOPLE along the Pony Express Trail who were invaluable sources for the information we needed to complete this book.

Those involved with state historic sites: Gary Chilcote, director of Patee House Museum; Duane Durst, Hollenberg Pony Express Station State Historic Site; Jeffrey Bargar, assistant superintendent of Rock Creek State Historical Park; Brady Hansen, Camp Floyd and Stagecoach Inn State Park; and James Prida, superintendent of Fort Churchill State Historic Park.

The following property owners kindly allowed us access to their lands to shoot photographs of Pony Express locations: Larry Gill, Jeanne Mahar, Rich and Mattie Wilmes, the Robert Eddy family, John Trowbridge, Olive Thompson, and M. Lillian Dixon.

Local historians who assisted us in our research: Dan Koch, Seneca, Kansas; Ken Martin, National Pony Express Association, Marysville, Kansas; the Curt Martin family, Farson, Wyoming; Sandra Allen, Utah Welcome Center; Billie J. Byrne Rightmire, Genoa New Courthouse Museum, Genoa, Nevada; Byron Clark, Carson City, Nevada; and Frank Tortorich, Jackson, California.

We couldn't do our work without the cooperation of the Bureau of Land Management employees. Those who aided us with information and maps: Tracy Pharo, Jerry Valentine, Greg Hill, Lowell Decker, Lewis Kirkman, and Mike Bunker. Special thanks to Craig Bromley, archeologist at the Lander, Wyoming, BLM office, who was especially helpful.

The staff at the Newport, Oregon, Public Library was diligent, and successful, in their search for the books we needed.

We greatly appreciate the help of Joseph R. Nardone, Pony Express Trail Association, and Jackie Lewin, curator of history, St. Joseph Museum, who were kind enough to impart some of their vast knowledge of the Pony Express to us. And using the maps in Greg Franzwa's excellent publications made following the trail easy.

Our thanks also to those at Mountain Press who were involved with the book, especially our editor, Gwen McKenna, and Kim Ericsson, who was responsible for the layout and design.

❊ NOTES TO THE READER ❊

MANY DISCREPANCIES EXIST in material concerning the Pony Express, and it's often difficult to prove anything one way or another regarding the stations, the riders, or the service itself. There is scant primary information to be found about the Pony Express because very few records exist from the company that ran the Pony Express, the Central Overland California & Pikes Peak Express Company. Much of the surviving information on the Pony Express comes from newspaper and magazine articles written while it was in operation in 1860 and 1861, and from a few books and articles written years later. This material often contains conflicting information.

Among these sources there is disagreement as to the number of stations, the names of some stations, and whether certain places were Pony Express stations at all. There are also differing opinions about which men were or were not riders, which riders made the longest or fastest run or took part in certain events. Because of the disparities, the text of this book may or may not agree with that of other publications.

To compile the photographs, we traveled the entire length of the Pony Express Trail several times. We found that some stations have been restored or rebuilt, and in a few places, in dry desert areas, ruins of actual stations exist. We have photographed the structures and ruins wherever possible, but in many instances we can show only the site where a station once stood.

Through these photographs and the accompanying text, we offer a concise history of the Pony Express that, we hope, will allow you to envision the dashing riders galloping across the country and vicariously share their adventures.

❧ SITES OF INTEREST ❧

IF YOU WANT TO EXPERIENCE the Pony Express Trail firsthand, you can use the following lists to find places to visit and sources of information about the trail.

Places to Visit

MISSOURI

Jefferson National
Expansion Memorial
Museum of Western Expansion
St. Louis, Missouri
314-655-1700
www.nps.gov/jeff

National Frontier Trails Center
Independence, Missouri
816-325-7575
www.frontiertrailscenter.com

Patee House Museum
St. Joseph, Missouri
816-232-8206
www.stjoseph.net/ponyexpress/

Pony Express Museum
St. Joseph, Missouri
800-530-5930
www.ponyexpress.org

St. Joseph Museum
St. Joseph, Missouri
800-530-8866
www.stjosephmuseum.org

KANSAS

Hollenberg Pony Express
Station State Historic Park
Hanover, Kansas
785-337-2635
www.kshs.org/places/hollenbg.htm

Original Pony Express Home Station
No. 1 Museum
Marysville, Kansas
785-562-3825

NEBRASKA

Chimney Rock National Historic Site
Bayard, Nebraska
308-568-2581
www.nebraskahistory.org

Durham Western Heritage Museum
Omaha, Nebraska
402-444-5071
www.dwhm.org

Fort Kearny State Historical Park
Kearney, Nebraska
308-234-9513
www.ngpc.state.ne.us/parks/
ftkearny.html

Gothenburg Pony Express Station
Gothenburg Nebraska
800-482-5520
www.ci.gothenburg.ne.us/
attractions_lodges.htm#pony

Museum of Nebraska History
Lincoln, Nebraska
800-833-6747
www.nebraskahistory.org

Rock Creek Station
State Historical Park
Fairbury, Nebraska
402-729-5777
www.ngpc.state.ne.us/parks/rcstat.html

Scotts Bluff National Monument
Gering, Nebraska
308-436-4340
www.nps.gov/scbl

COLORADO
Fort Sedgewick Depot Museum
Julesburg, Colorado
970-474-2061
www.kci.net/~history

WYOMING
Fort Bridger State Historic Site
Fort Bridger, Wyoming
307-782-3842
http://commerce.state.wy.us/sphs/
bridger.htm

Fort Laramie National Historic Site
Fort Laramie, Wyoming
307-837-2221
www.nps.fov/fola

National Historic Trails
Interpretive Center
Casper, Wyoming
307-261-7700
www.wy.blm.gov/nhtic

UTAH
Camp Floyd and Stagecoach
Inn State Park
Fairfield, Utah
801-768-8932
www.stateparks.utah.gov

NEVADA
Churchill County
Museum and Archives
Fallon, Nevada
775-423-3677
www.ccmuseum.org

Eureka Sentinel Museum
Eureka, Nevada
775-237-5010
www.eurekasentinelmuseum.eurekanu.org

Fort Churchill State Historic Park
Silver Springs, Nevada
775-577-2347
www.state.nv.us/stparks

Genoa Courthouse Museum
Genoa, Nevada
775-782-4325
www.carsonvalleymuseums.com

Mormon Station State Historical Park
Genoa, Nevada
775-782-2590
www.state.nv.us/stparks

Nevada State Museum
Carson City, Nevada
775-687-4810
www.nevadaculture.org

Northeast Nevada Museum
Elko, Nevada
775-738-3418
www.nenv-museum.org

White Pine Historical Museum
Ely, Nevada
775-289-4710
www.webpanda.com/
white_pine_county/historical_society/
pony_exp.htm

CALIFORNIA
Old Sacramento Visitors'
    Information Center
Sacramento, California
916-442-7644
www.oldsacramento.com

Local Information Sources

Austin Chamber of Commerce
Austin, Nevada
775-964-2200
www.austin.igate.com

Carson City Chamber of Commerce
Carson City, Nevada
775-882-1565
www.carsoncitychamber.com

Casper Area Convention
    and Visitors' Bureau
Casper, Wyoming
800-852-1889
www.casperwyoming.org/visitors

Eureka County
    Chamber of Commerce
Eureka, Nevada
775-237-5484
www.co.eureka.nv.us

Fallon Convention and
    Tourism Authority
Fallon, Nevada
775-423-4556
www.fallonchamber.com

Folsom Chamber of Commerce
Folsom, California
800-377-1414
www.folsomchamber.com

White Pine Chamber of Commerce
Ely, Nevada
775-289-8877
www.elynevada.net

Bureau of Land Management Offices

Carson City Field Office
Carson City, Nevada
775-885-6000

Ely Office
Ely, Nevada
775-289-1800

Salt Lake District Office
Pony Express Resources Area
Salt Lake City, Utah
801-977-4300

Wyoming Historic Trails Office
Casper, Wyoming
307-261-7600
Lander, Wyoming
307-332-8400

Web site for all offices:
www.blm.gov/nhpl/index.htm

General Information Sources

National Pony Express Association
P.O. Box 236
Pollock Pines, California 95762
916-622-5205
www.xphomestation.com/npea.html

Pony Express Trail Association
139 San Antonio Way
Sacramento, California 95819
949-855-3248

www.americanwest.com/trails/pages/
    ponyexp1.htm

www.nps.gov/poex

www.sfmuseum.org/hist1/pxpress.html

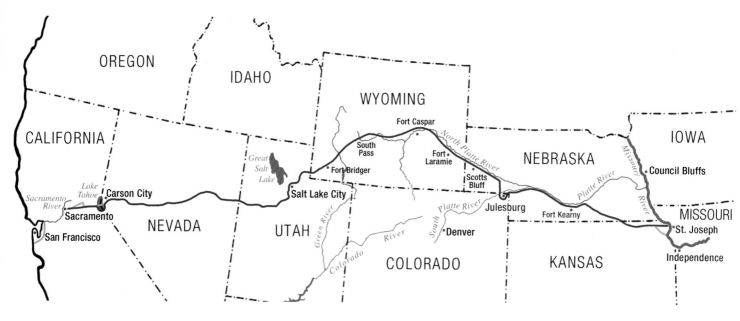

1
❀ DEVELOPMENT ❀
of the Pony Express

IN THE MID-NINETEENTH CENTURY, mail delivery was relatively regular and swift as far west as Missouri, but it was slow and erratic beyond there, especially to distant California. By 1860, with a civil war seeming inevitable, the citizens of California, who by then numbered 380,000, wanted news and they wanted it quickly.

The earliest California settlers received their mail by steamship. The route was around Cape Horn, the southernmost tip of South America, and it often took months for the mail to arrive. Many congressmen thought an overland mail system might speed up delivery. So in 1851, Major George Chorpenning and Samuel H. Woodson each signed a contract to provide a portion of the first overland mail-delivery service. Chorpenning's service carried the mail once a month between California and Salt Lake City; Woodson's company had the contract for the route

between Salt Lake City and Independence, Missouri. The overland delivery, made by pack mule, was faster than the steamships, but it still took three to four weeks for the mail to arrive.

Over the next few years, while Chorpenning continued delivering the mail, Congress debated which of two main routes to California should be used. Chorpenning was using the central, or Salt Lake, route between St. Joseph, Missouri, and San Francisco. It ran more or less across the middle of the country, spanning just under two thousand miles and crossing the formidable Rocky Mountains and Sierra Nevada. The southern route stretched between St. Louis and San Francisco via Little Rock, El Paso, Yuma (Arizona), and San Diego. Nearly 2,800 miles long, this trail was known as the Oxbow Route because of its great swoop to the south, and also as the Butterfield

Route because it was the same route the Butterfield stagecoach line had been using for many years.

In 1857 the Northerners in Congress hoped that the government would continue to use Chorpenning's central route, reasoning that it would be less likely to be disrupted in the event of war. But the postmaster, a Southerner from Tennessee, awarded the mail contract to John Butterfield. Although the southern route was hundreds of miles longer than the central route, Butterfield's stages averaged delivery times of twenty-three to twenty-five days, close to those of Chorpenning. Nevertheless, anxious Californians clamored for faster service.

The time was ripe to put into action a plan that had formed in the mind of William H. Russell, senior partner in the firm of Russell, Majors & Waddell. Since 1854, Russell and his partners, Alexander Majors and William B. Waddell, had run a freighting operation along the Oregon and Santa Fe Trails, so they were experienced in hauling goods by wagon. But what Russell conceived was something quite different. Instead of using wagons, stagecoaches, or pack mules to carry the mail, his idea was to use relays of swift riders on horses. With the system of stations he envisioned, and with the couriers riding around the clock carrying light loads of only letters, telegrams, and newspapers, he reckoned that the trip could be made in ten days.

Russell's conservative partners were less than enthusiastic about his proposal, but they reluctantly agreed to give it a try. Thus, on January 27, 1860, the Pony Express was established. It would be a division of the Central Overland California & Pikes Peak Express Company, which the partners had formed in 1859 to carry mail and freight. When the service started, riders departed from St. Joseph and Sacramento once a week, but soon departures increased to twice weekly.

Russell, Majors & Waddell established the headquarters of the Pony Express at Patee House, a large hotel in St. Joseph with a livery stable three blocks away. The company selected St. Joseph for two primary reasons: it had telegraph service from the East, and it was the western terminus of the Hannibal & St. Joseph Railroad, which ran across Missouri and connected with eastern rail lines.

The firm set to work designating and building stations, buying horses, and recruiting riders and station personnel. Russell's plan included dividing the route into five divisions. The company appointed Benjamin F. Ficklin to be the general superintendent over the entire route and hired the five division superintendents: A. E. Lewis was the superintendent for Division One, between St. Joseph and Fort Kearny, Nebraska; Division Two, between Fort Kearny and Horseshoe Creek Station in Wyoming, was under Joseph A. "Jack" Slade; James E. Bromley supervised Division Three, between Horseshoe Station and Salt Lake City; Division Four, between Salt Lake City and Roberts Creek Station in Nevada, was under Howard Egan; and Bolivar Roberts handled Division Five, between Roberts Creek and Sacramento.

The Stations

The Pony Express used fifteen of the company's existing stage stations from St. Joseph, Missouri, to Julesburg, Colorado. These were spaced twenty-five to thirty miles apart. Fifteen more stations were added at approximately halfway points between the existing ones. Farther west, the company purchased or leased some existing stage stations and built new ones so there would be no more than fifteen miles between stops, the distance that horses could travel at top speed without a rest.

Patee House, St. Joseph, Missouri, headquarters of the Pony Express

The completed route included about 154 stations, the number and location of which varied during the Pony Express's existence because of route changes, destruction of buildings in Indian raids, and the use of temporary and alternate stops. (See Appendix A for a list of stations used at one time or another.) Some were home

3

stations, located seventy-five to one hundred miles apart, where riders stopped to eat and sleep at the end of their route. The others were relay stations, where riders just changed mounts.

Topography was an important factor in determining the placement of stations and the distance between them. It also determined the materials used in the stations' construction. Where timber was available, mainly at the eastern and western ends of the line, stations were built of wood. In desert areas, adobe was generally used. Some stations on the grassy prairies in Nebraska were made of sod. A few were constructed of available stones and rocks, and some were nothing more than a dugout in the side of a hill. Regardless of their building materials, most stations were crude structures with few amenities.

The Horses

The firm purchased about five hundred horses at $150 to $200 each. On average, the horses were fourteen hands high and weighed about nine hundred pounds, so the Pony Express mounts were not really ponies. For the eastern divisions, which crossed the prairies and plains between St. Joseph and Fort Laramie, the partners acquired blooded stock from Kentucky and

Tack shop in the Pony Express Stables, St. Joseph, Missouri

the Missouri Valley—horses known for their swiftness. For western divisions, with more difficult terrain, they selected horses for stamina rather than speed and purchased strong, resilient mustangs. All Pony

Pony Express office in the Patee House

Pony Express Stables

Blacksmith shop in the Pony Express Stables

Express mounts had to be superior animals—in summer, they had to average ten miles an hour with no stops between relay stations; in winter, when conditions warranted, the average was reduced to eight miles an hour. With horses running in relays around the clock, the mail traveled, on average, about 220 miles each day in the eastern divisions and about 160 miles a day in the western areas.

The Riders

Initially, Russell, Majors & Waddell hired about sixty riders, all experienced horsemen. Most weighed about 125 pounds and were around age twenty, although some were much younger; one was supposedly eleven years old. The pay was about $120 a month plus room and board, but riders whose routes went through especially dangerous territory received $150 a month. Before a rider was accepted, he had to sign an oath attesting that he was of good moral character and not addicted to drink. Upon signing, the rider was presented with a small Bible.

Each rider was assigned a route between two home stations, riding in one direction on one run and going the opposite way on the next one. He changed mounts at relay stations, which were about ten to fifteen miles apart. When the rider arrived at a station, he was allowed only two minutes to change mounts. Some riders could make the change in as little as fifteen seconds. So there would be no delay, stationkeepers were required to have the remount saddled and bridled half an hour before the rider was scheduled to arrive. Sometimes when a rider arrived at his home station, he would find his replacement ill or incapacitated and would have to ride the next route as well, without a rest.

The Equipment

The riders' garb was typically a buckskin shirt, ordinary trousers tucked into high leather boots, and a slouch hat. All wore spurs and carried a quirt along with a revolver—usually a small Colt pistol—and an extra loaded cylinder. At first, the riders were also equipped with a bowie knife and a rifle, but soon these were eliminated because of the extra weight. Each rider was also issued a horn for signaling the stations that he was arriving.

Riders were expected not to use their weapons unless compelled to do so. Parts of the route went through sparsely settled, desolate land where Indians—many from tribes hostile to whites—lived and traveled. In case of trouble, help might be long in coming because there were only four military posts along the entire route. The riders were instructed to depend on speed to avoid danger. This usually worked, because the grain-fed, well-cared-for Pony Express horses could easily outdistance the grass-fed Indian ponies.

The typical western saddle was deemed too heavy for the Pony Express, so most riders used the lighter Spanish saddle favored by vaqueros. The stirrups were made of light wood and often fitted with *tapaderos*, leather coverings that protected the rider's legs.

The mail was secured in four *cantinas*—weatherproof, padlocked leather boxes—which were attached to the corners of a heavy piece of leather called a *mochila*. The mochila was laid over the saddle and held in place by the rider's weight. It had a hole in front to go over the saddle horn and a slit in back that fit over the cantle. This design permitted the mochila to be swept off the horse and onto the remount quickly.

Two cantinas hung in front of the rider's legs and two hung behind. Three

A mochila, in which the mail was carried, fit over the saddle. (Hollenberg Pony Express Station State Historic Park)

of them carried mail going through to the eastern or western terminus; these were locked before the rider departed the terminus, and only the stationkeeper at the other end of the line could open them. The fourth cantina, on the front left side, was the "way pocket," for mail picked up and delivered along the route and for waybills listing times of arrival and departure. It could be unlocked by home stationkeepers.

Weights and Rates

The saddle and mochila with empty cantinas weighed about thirteen pounds. Russell set the maximum weight of mail at twenty pounds—the weight of about six hundred letters—though the average was fifteen pounds. To keep the weight to a minimum, most letter writers used a tissuelike paper, and even newspapers, which comprised two-thirds of the Pony Express business, were printed on special thin paper. The company continued to carry packages and heavier mail on pack mules.

At first, it cost five dollars to send a half-ounce letter by Pony Express, but rates gradually dropped. By July 1861 the rate was one dollar per half ounce. In addition to the service charge, customers had to purchase a special envelope for ten cents.

The First Ride

On April 3, 1860, just two months and a few days after the establishment of the Pony Express, the service was ready for the first rider to depart. St. Joseph was decked out in bunting, a brass band was playing, and people thronged the streets hours before five o'clock that afternoon, when the great event was scheduled to happen. However, it didn't come off as planned. A special messenger carrying the first mail for the Pony Express left Washington, D. C., by rail on March 30. After a short stop in New York City to pick up more mail, he continued westward by train but missed his connection in Detroit, which threw off the rest of the schedule. As soon as J. T. K. Haywood, superintendent of the Hannibal & St. Joseph Railroad, heard about the delay, he ordered a special train, made up of an engine and one car, to wait in Hannibal, Missouri, until the messenger arrived, after which it was to depart instantly. George H. Davis, roadmaster of the line, ordered the main track cleared of all trains and every switch spiked.

The fearless Addison Clark, one of the railroad's best engineers, fired up the locomotive *Missouri* and was ready to go. The messenger arrived about two and a half hours late. As soon as he boarded the

Locomotive of the Hannibal & St. Joseph Railroad, built circa 1860 (Pattee House Museum)

waiting train, Clark pulled the throttle all the way back and was off. Although the train barreled along at up to sixty miles an hour, Clark couldn't make up the time. The crowd in St. Joseph had to wait more than two hours before hearing the shrill whistle announcing the locomotive's arrival. During the wait, Alexander Majors and the mayor of St. Joseph made speeches. Majors's speech was prophetic in that it forecast that the Pony Express would in time be supplanted by the "tireless iron horse." After the speeches, a cannon in front of Patee House fired a salute, and at 7:15 P.M. the rider was off to the west.

On the same day, a rider left San Francisco heading east. He rode a short distance to the dock where the steamboat *Antelope* was waiting to take him up the Sacramento River to Sacramento. In Sacramento, another rider was waiting at the wharf to pick up the mochila and ride off on the first leg of the overland run.

It is not known for certain who was really the first rider out of St. Joseph. Much evidence points to William "Billy" Richardson, although some sources indicate that John Frye was the first. (See Appendix B, The First Westbound Rider.) On the first eastbound trip, James Randall carried the mail from San Francisco to Sacramento on the steamer. Historians differ about the identity of the first rider from Sacramento, but most sources cite Sam Hamilton as having the honor.

The first trip westward was completed in nine days, twenty-three hours. The eastbound trip was made in exactly ten days—more than twice as fast as any stagecoach could do.

2
✸ KANSAS ✸
Stations and Stories

In Kansas Territory, the Pony Express route started on the west side of the Missouri River, opposite St. Joseph. After it left the bluffs along the river, the route went generally northwest through rolling prairie lands laced with springs and creeks, which commonly supported stands of hardwoods.

Elwood

The town of Elwood, Kansas, was only five miles from St. Joseph, Missouri. Because riders didn't change horses there, Elwood was not a true relay station, but it figured in one of the longest rides. Perhaps because of a wager, rider J. H. "Jack" Keetley rode east from Big Sandy Station in Nebraska to Elwood, picked up the waiting mail, and then rode back over a portion of the route that he had just traversed to Seneca Station. Keetley claimed that he completed this ride of about three hundred miles in just under twenty-four hours.

Troy Station

The first designated relay station was fifteen miles from St. Joseph in Troy, Kansas. Troy Station consisted of a hotel and a barn that could accommodate five horses.

Troy was along the route of Johnny Frye, who was quite a ladies' man. Some of the girls who lived along his route baked sweets and held them out to him as he rode by. The girls noticed that he had trouble holding the cookies with his one free hand. To solve the problem, they began baking cookies with a hole in the center so that he could slip them on his fingers. Thus, supposedly, was born the doughnut.

One of the girls was so taken with Johnny that she wanted his red necktie to include in a quilt she was making. Johnny wouldn't give up his favorite tie, so she decided to steal it from him as he rode through on one of his trips. As he came into view, she was ready and waiting on her horse. While she galloped alongside him, she tried unsuccessfully to pull the tie from his neck. As Johnny began to pull ahead, she made another grab for the tie and got hold of his shirttail instead. A piece of it tore off, and this was the memento of Johnny Frye that ended up in her quilt.

Kennekuk Station

Forty-four miles from St. Joseph, Kennekuk, Kansas, was a good-sized settlement with two large hotels, numerous stores and businesses, and many houses. Kennekuk Station, run by Tom Perry and his wife, was the first home station west of St. Joseph. It also served as a stage station. Among the services the Perrys provided to stage passengers were meals accompanied by their renowned coffee. Mark Twain was one of the notables who sampled Mrs. Perry's coffee and good cooking.

Seneca Station

Seneca Station, in the Smith Hotel in Seneca, Kansas, was the next home station west of Kennekuk. John Smith ran the station, and his wife did the cooking. In the settlement, Levi Hensel maintained a blacksmith shop, and the Pony Express made use of his services. He was so good

Pony Express crossing of the South Fork of the Big Nemaha River at Seneca Pony Express Station, Seneca, Kansas

Stagecoach swales at site of Guittard's Pony Express Station, north of Beattie, Kansas

at his craft that people came from long distances to have him shoe their horses.

David Robert Jay, one rider on the route between Seneca Station and Big Sandy Station in Nebraska, was hired after walking nearly sixty miles from his home in Manhattan, Kansas, to Marysville to apply for the job. He was not yet fourteen years old at the time.

Guittard's Station

During the life of the Pony Express, Guittard's Station, on Vermillion Creek, was at different times both a home station and a relay station. It also was a stage station. The facility had a barn with space for twenty-four horses. Unlike many of the stations, this one was well kept and clean.

One of the riders on this route, Will Boulton, was older than most riders—in his thirties—when he was hired. But that didn't prevent him from doing his job. During one of his runs, his horse was injured five miles from Guittard's Station. Boulton unloaded the horse and, carrying the mochila and all his equipment, walked to the station, picked up another horse, and finished his ride.

Marysville Station

The established town of Marysville, Kansas, on the Big Blue River, was selected to be the site of a home station. The Pony Express facility had no living accommodations—it was just a livery stable with a blacksmith shop—so the riders stayed at the nearby American Hotel.

Riders generally forded most of the streams and rivers along their routes, but

Restored Pony Express home station, Marysville, Kansas

14

Hollenberg Pony Express Station State Historic Site (Cottonwood Station), Hanover, Kansas

at Marysville, when the Big Blue River was flooded and swollen beyond its usual depth of two and a half feet, they used a ferry operated by Robert Shibley.

About eight miles west of Marysville, the Pony Express route joined the path worn earlier by thousands of emigrants, the Oregon Trail.

Cottonwood Station

After prospecting in California, Australia, and Peru, German emigrant G. H. Hollenberg returned to Kansas and established Cottonwood Station, which consisted of a large ranch house and a huge stable. His family's quarters, a store, and a post office were on the first floor of the house. Pony Express riders and stage drivers, as well as his own six employees, slept in the second-floor loft. Hollenberg's store supplied food, clothing, livestock, livestock feed, and other items to emigrants heading west on the Oregon Trail.

3
❧ NEBRASKA & COLORADO ❧
Stations and Stories

PONY EXPRESS RIDERS in Nebraska Territory faced a route that covered vast, mostly treeless prairies. Settlements were few and consisted mainly of widely spaced trading posts and forts. Indians were the main inhabitants of the land.

Rock Creek Station

In 1857 S. C. Glenn established a ranch on the west side of Rock Creek and built a station to cater to stages, freight lines, and emigrants on the Oregon Trail. In 1859 David McCanles bought the place. Because of a lack of good water at the original station, McCanles built a new one with a good well on the east bank of the creek. Later, to eliminate the difficult ford, he built a toll bridge over the steep-sided creek. In 1860 McCanles sold the property to Russell, Majors & Waddell.

In 1861, when the company fell behind in its payments, McCanles, accompanied by his twelve-year-old son Monroe and two of his employees, all unarmed, went to stationkeeper Horace Wellman's house to find out when he would get his money. Wellman wouldn't see McCanles and sent his stable hand, James Butler Hickok, to answer the door. Hickok knew McCanles and didn't like him because McCanles had made fun of Hickok's buckteeth and protruding upper lip, calling him "Duck Bill."

McCanles, suspecting that Wellman was hiding, moved to another door of the cabin to look for him. There Hickok shot him. McCanles's two hired hands, who were near the stable, heard the gunshot and ran toward the cabin. Hickok shot them too. Both wounded, they tried to run away, but Hickok and Wellman caught them and finished them off. Hickok and Wellman also tried to kill young Monroe, who had seen everything, but he managed to escape.

*Reconstruction of David McCanles's toll bridge over Rock Creek,
Rock Creek State Historical Park, Fairbury, Nebraska*

*Stable, East Ranch,
Rock Creek State
Historical Park*

*East Ranch House
and corner of
bunkhouse, Rock Creek
State Historical Park*

Wellman and Hickok were arrested for the crime but were acquitted on grounds of self-defense against the McCanles "gang." Hickok's nickname "Duck Bill," misheard as "Dutch Bill," eventually became "Wild Bill," a name that persists to this day. (See Appendix B, James Butler "Wild Bill" Hickok.)

Big Sandy Station

Big Sandy was a home station about twelve miles west of Rock Creek Station, where the wagon road from Nebraska City joined the Oregon Trail. Travelers always hoped to catch sight of the dashing Pony Express riders, and the riders usually put on a good show. A young mule driver on a wagon train, approaching Big Sandy, described a Pony Express rider as "racing and whooping" past the train and panicking the mules.

Thirty-two Mile Creek Station

Thirty-two Mile Creek Station took its name from the creek on which it stood, thirty-two miles east of Fort Kearny. These miles were on the route of rider Melville Baughn. Once while Baughn was on a layover at the fort, someone stole his horse. He tracked the thief, found the horse, and returned to the fort in time to take the next mail back to Thirty-two Mile Creek Station.

Summit Station

Summit Station, which served as both a Pony Express relay station and a stage station, was merely a dugout, extending three feet above and four feet under the ground. Dugouts were not unusual structures on the prairie. This country was also home to many animals, including the buffalo, which roamed the land in vast herds.

Kearny Station

Kearny Station, a home station, was a few miles east of the fort of the same name. The adventures of William Campbell, who rode between Kearny Station and Cottonwood Springs Station, typify what many Pony Express riders encountered.

Like all riders, Campbell had to carry the mail no matter what the weather. One time, Campbell had to ride through a blizzard with zero-degree temperatures and snowdrifts as tall as he was. In the daylight he kept to the trail by following tall weeds; after dark he relied on his horse to find the way. When the weary Campbell reached his home station, he found no replacement rider and had to take the mail another fifteen miles to the next station.

One night Campbell rode by a pack of wolves feeding on the carcass of a buffalo. Although wolves usually avoid humans, for some reason they abandoned their

20

Buffalo

meal and started chasing Campbell. He was several miles from the station and didn't have his revolver. As the wolves gained on him, he blew his horn, which startled them and momentarily halted their pursuit. Sounding his horn several more times, Campbell managed to reach the station before the animals caught up with him. The next day, Campbell laced a dead ox with poison, hauled it about a mile away from the station, and left it for his previous night's tormenters. Later he found a dozen or so dead wolves near the carcass. He skinned them and sold the pelts.

In another incident, Campbell got lost one black night after a bad thunderstorm. He could hear the Platte River flowing nearby but could not see it. As he always carried a lariat, the resourceful rider threw one end of the rope into the water. From the direction of the rope's pull, Campbell could tell which way the river was flowing and got his bearings.

Fort Kearny

In addition to being a military post, bustling Fort Kearny was a Pony Express station and a stage stop. It was also a place where emigrants on the Oregon Trail camped.

Fort Kearny was on the route of Alexander Toponce. He, like many other

Cottonwood trees (planted 1848), Fort Kearny State Historical Park, Kearny, Nebraska

riders, occasionally engaged in a practice to speed up the mail. If upon arriving at the station where he was to pick up the eastbound mail, for example, he found

Fort Kearny State Historical Park

that the rider was late, Toponce would ride west, taking another horse along. When he met the eastbound rider, they exchanged mochilas and Toponce gave the rider the extra, fresh horse. Then Toponce turned around and rode east while the other rider turned around and rode west. This maneuver kept the mail moving and left no mail sitting at a station waiting for a rider to pick it up.

Willow Island Station

Willow Island Station was a relay station with, according to journalist Sir Richard Burton, on his stagecoach trip through the West in 1860, a "drinking shop" on the premises. Perhaps Burton partook of the spirits, but the Pony Express riders never did, in obedience to their oath.

Midway Station

Midway Station was a home station for rider James Moore. His route ran 140 miles between Midway and Julesburg (just over the present-day Nebraska state line in Colorado), significantly longer than the 75- to 100-mile average. Once, his mochila contained westbound army dispatches marked "urgent." Suspecting that they pertained to trouble brewing with the Indians, he rode hard and reached Julesburg in eleven hours—the trip normally took at least fourteen. When he arrived, he found the eastbound rider too ill to carry the mail, which had just arrived, back to Midway. Moore gulped down some coffee, crammed his pockets with food, jumped into the saddle, and was off again over the 140 miles that he had just covered. He made the round trip in just twenty-two hours.

Machette's Station

Machette's Station was one of the buildings comprising the vast Upper 96 Ranch, owned by a man named Williams. The log structure, which served as a trading post and ranch house, was built in 1854 by Sam Machette. (See Appendix A.)

Eleven miles west of the next station, Cottonwood Springs, is the beginning of the Platte River, formed by the joining of the North and South Platte Rivers. The Pony Express route followed the South Platte between here and Julesburg, Colorado.

24

Willow Island Pony Express Station, moved to Cozad, Nebraska,
from its original location near Lexington, Nebraska

Midway Pony Express Station, south of Gothenberg, Nebraska

*Machette's Pony Express Station, moved to Gothenberg, Nebraska,
from its original location southwest of Brady, Nebraska.
Originally a two-story structure, only one story was restored.*

O'Fallon's Bluff, with wagon rims commemorating the Oregon Trail, southeast of Sutherland, Nebraska

O'Fallon's Bluff Station

The north side of O'Fallon's Bluff stands at the edge of the South Platte River. The landscape here was ideal for Indian ambushes, so Oregon Trail emigrants blazed a trail over the top of the bluff. Pony Express riders also used this trail. The station was west of the bluff.

Diamond Springs Station

Although just twenty-six miles east of the home station of Julesburg, Diamond Springs Station also served as a home station at one point.

The Pony Express route, which followed the Oregon Trail from Kansas through most of Nebraska, departed from it a few miles west of Diamond Springs Station. There, most emigrants crossed the South Platte River at what was called the Lower California Crossing, but the Pony Express riders crossed about twenty miles farther west, at the Upper California Crossing, about two miles west of Julesburg, in Colorado Territory. Here the trail cut north, back into Nebraska, to the North Platte River, where it again joined the Oregon Trail.

Julesburg Station (Colorado)

Julesburg Station was one of only two Pony Express stations in Colorado, both in the far northeast corner of the territory. The other was Frontz's, or South Platte, Station, east of Julesburg.

Situated on the road to Denver, the town of Julesburg was a bustling place. A shady character named Jules Reni operated a trading post and stage station that later served as a Pony Express station. Reni's establishment was headquarters for out-

Site of Diamond Springs Pony Express Station, Brule, Nebraska. The lighter areas in the grass mark the foundations of the original building.

laws, horse thieves, and cutthroats. The year before the Pony Express was organized, the Central Overland California & Pikes Peak Express Company sent Benjamin Ficklin to clean up Julesburg. With the help of Jack Slade, later a division superintendent, Ficklin eventually ran Reni out of town, and the place lost its notorious reputation.

*Pony Express crossing of the South Platte River (upper California Crossing),
near Julesburg, Colorado*

Pole Creek Number 3 Station

A few Pony Express stations, mostly the eastern ones, were clean and had decent accommodations and food, but many were rude structures with few amenities. Commonly they fit Sir Richard Burton's description of the Pole Creek Number 3 Pony Express and stage station, where he and his fellow stage passengers stopped for a noon meal. Burton wrote that on Lodgepole Creek stood a "hovel" with mud walls, the ceiling a "fine festoon-work of soot, and the floor was much like the ground outside, only not nearly so clean."

Mud Springs Station

Although Mud Springs was a Pony Express home station, it wasn't a much better place than Pole Creek Number 3 Station. One stage passenger described the sod structure roofed with poles, brush, and earth as a "dirty hovel, serving tough antilope [sic] steaks, fried on a filthy stove, with wooden boxes serving as chairs at a bench like table." In spite of the station's accommodations, the springs were a welcome sight to travelers who had just come miles across the dry and dusty lands that stretched east and west beyond the station.

Spring at Mud Springs Pony Express Station site,
southeast of Bridgeport, Nebraska

Courthouse Rock Station

Except for a few low hills, most of the prairie along the Pony Express route was featureless. But in western Nebraska, the great sandstone formations of Courthouse and Jail Rocks were visible for miles. The Oregon Trail skirted the formations on the north side, while the Pony Express route passed them on the south. The station was just southwest of Courthouse Rock.

Courthouse and Jail Rocks, south of Bridgeport, Nebraska

Chimney Rock Station

As with Courthouse and Jail Rocks, Chimney Rock was easy to spot from far away. The station's precise location is not known, but a logical place for it would have been at Facus Springs, about three miles east of the formation, near where the Pony Express route rejoined the Oregon Trail.

Chimney Rock National Historic Site, Bayard, Nebraska

Scott's Bluff, Scotts Bluff National Monument, Gering, Nebraska

Scott's Bluff Station

Dominating the landscape at Scott's Bluff Station was the massive bluff for which it was named. Mitchell Pass cuts through the rock formation of which Scott's Bluff is a part. The Pony Express station was about two and a half miles northwest of the pass, near where the North Platte River flows close to the base of the bluff.

36

Oregon Trail and Pony Express route below Eagle Rock, Scotts Bluff National Monument

Mitchell Pass, Scotts Bluff National Monument

On Mark Twain's stagecoach journey from Missouri to Nevada, he expected to see a Pony Express rider, but he had come as far as western Nebraska without seeing one. Then, near Scott's Bluff Station, Twain heard his stage driver shout "Here he comes!" Twain said that at first he saw only a black speck on the horizon, but shortly it became defined as a horse and rider. Almost as soon as they heard the hoofbeats, the waving rider passed the stage. It happened so quickly that Twain likened it to "a flash of unreal fancy" as the rider went "winging away like a belated fragment of a storm."

Fort Laramie National Historic Site, west of Fort Laramie, Wyoming

4
❈ WYOMING ❈
Stations and Stories

IN WYOMING TERRITORY, the Pony Express route went through mostly arid land. Even when the trail reached the Continental Divide at South Pass, in the Rocky Mountains, the landscape was not typical of mountain areas but was treeless and covered mainly with sagebrush, just like the terrain on either side of the divide. It was in Wyoming that the trail reached its highest elevation, after climbing steadily westward from 823 feet above sea level at St. Joseph to 7,412 feet at South Pass.

Sutler's store, Fort Laramie National Historic Site

Interior of sutler's store

Fort Laramie Station

First established in 1834 as a trading post by the mountain man Bill Sublette, Fort Laramie became a military outpost in 1849. Pony Express riders regularly stopped at the sutler's store there to pick up and deliver mail, but the actual Pony Express station was probably just west of the fort.

Ward's Station

Ward's Station was just thirteen hundred feet west of the famous Oregon Trail landmark Register Cliff, upon which many emigrants carved their names.

Register Cliff State Historic Site, Guernsey, Wyoming

Cottonwood Station

Cottonwood Station stood at the crossing of Cottonwood Creek. The creek was usually dry, but after a heavy rain it could run ten feet deep.

Horseshoe Creek Station

Division superintendent Jack Slade, who had aided Benjamin F. Ficklin in the cleanup of Julesburg, Colorado, lived with his family at Horseshoe Creek Station. He kept strict control over his division and had a reputation for being ruthless and quick to use his gun.

One day, just after rider Henry Avis finished his route at Horseshoe Creek Station, word arrived that a Sioux war party had been seen at Deer Creek Station, to the west. Upon hearing this, the rider who was to take the mail west refused to go, so Avis rode in his place.

When he arrived at Deer Creek Station, Avis found that Indians had raided it and driven off all the stock. Because of the Indian problem, the eastbound rider due to leave from there also refused to make his run. Again Avis took on the ride. He made it safely back to Horseshoe Creek Station, after traveling a total of 220 miles. The company rewarded him with a $300 bonus.

Horseshoe Creek near the site of the Pony Express station, northwest of Glendo, Wyoming

*Laramie Peak near Cottonwood Pony Express Station,
west of Glendo, Wyoming. Dark streaks are old wagon ruts.*

La Bonte Station

La Bonte Station, a stagecoach station on the bank of La Bonte Creek, became a Pony Express stop in August 1860 due to a change in the route. The station included a sturdy corral, which also served as a stockade for protection from Indian attacks, and a brush wickiup to house the stationkeepers.

La Bonte Creek crossing, south of Douglas, Wyoming

La Prele Station

A stage and Pony Express station, La Prele Station was built on a well-timbered creek, so wood, water, and grass for grazing animals were abundant. A mile to the southwest, an impressive natural bridge spanned the creek.

*Ayres Natural Bridge over La Prele Creek, upstream of La Prele
Pony Express Station, southwest of Douglas, Wyoming*

Reconstructed section of the bridge over the North Platte River
at Platte Bridge Pony Express Station,
Fort Caspar State Historic Site, Casper, Wyoming

Platte Bridge Station

Riders reached Platte Bridge Station, also a stage stop, by a thousand-foot-long bridge over the North Platte River. Louis Guenot, the stage stationkeeper, built the bridge and the station in 1859, at a cost of $40,000.

Red Buttes Station

As early as 1812, trappers had used the crossing of the North Platte River at Bessemer Bend, where Red Buttes Station was eventually established. The station, which had been an old trading post, stood on a bench above the river, safely above floodwaters.

Buttes at Red Buttes Pony Express Station, west of Casper, Wyoming

Bessemer Bend crossing of the
North Platte River at Red Buttes Station

Red Buttes was the home station for a fifteen-year-old rider named William Frederick "Billy" Cody, later known as Buffalo Bill. It was from here in 1861 that Cody made one of the most famous rides in Pony Express history.

Cody's regular route, which ran seventy-seven miles between Red Buttes and Three Crossings Stations, was a dangerous one through rough, desolate terrain and included a treacherous, wide, deep ford of the North Platte River. Hostile Indians, horse thieves, and sometimes bandits frequented the area. Once, after arriving at Three Crossings, Cody found that the rider who was to have taken the mail west had been killed the night before. The boy wasted no time in changing mounts and set off, riding thirty-six miles farther to St. Mary's Station. There, without pausing, he picked up the eastbound mail and rode all the way back to Red Buttes Station.

Cody rode a total of 226 miles that day and, by maintaining a speed of fifteen miles an hour, arrived on schedule at each of the stops along the way. (See Appendix B, William Frederick "Buffalo Bill" Cody.)

Spring at the site of Willow Springs Pony Express Station, west of Casper, Wyoming

Willow Springs Station

At Willow Springs, the combination stage and Pony Express station consisted of only a small, rough shed and no corral. The place, however, had abundant water and grass.

Independence Rock State Historic Site and the Sweetwater River, west of Alcova, Wyoming

Sweetwater Station

Sweetwater Station stood less than a mile east of the mammoth granite formation known as Independence Rock. The rock got its name from early trappers who camped there on the Fourth of July. The base of the rock, at the edge of the Sweetwater River, was a much-used camping spot for Oregon Trail emigrants, and some of them left a record of their visit by writing or carving their names on the rock.

In mid-September 1860, Indians raided this area frequently. In one incident at Sweetwater Station, they killed a man and took all the stock. The station was closed until it and other stations in the vicinity could be restocked with horses.

Looking east from the top of Independence Rock to the site of Sweetwater Pony Express Station

Plant's Station

Plant's Station was one of the relay stops where William Cody changed horses on his famous ride. Between Sweetwater Station and here, riders passed the curious rock formation known as Devil's Gate.

Devil's Gate and the Sweetwater River, west of Alcova, Wyoming

Split Rock Station

Split Rock Station, like so many of the stations, got its name from a nearby natural feature. In this case, it was a low mountain in the Rattlesnake Range with a noticeable cleft at the top. This landmark could be seen from many miles away.

60

Split Rock at the site of Split Rock Pony Express Station, east of Jeffrey City, Wyoming

Three Crossings Station

The settlement at Three Crossings included a Pony Express home station and a separate stage facility, both managed by the Moores, a Mormon family from England. The place got its name because emigrant wagons had to zigzag across the narrow, rocky Sweetwater River defile three times to find places on the banks wide enough to accommodate them.

*The Sweetwater River near Three Crossings Pony Express Station,
northeast of Jeffrey City, Wyoming*

Ice Slough Station

Ice Slough Station had a unique treat to offer people who stopped there: ice. Under the shallow water in the slough was an insulating layer of turf, and beneath the turf was ice that never thawed. Anyone who wanted a cold drink merely had to dig down about eight to ten inches to reach the ice.

Ice Slough, at site of Ice Slough Pony Express Station, west of Jeffrey City, Wyoming

St. Mary's Station

St. Mary's Station stood at six thousand feet above sea level in a meadow surrounded by rough and broken country. This was the turnaround point on William Cody's long ride. He may have been happy that he didn't have to linger there because, according to Sir Richard Burton, the place was a "terrible unclean hole" and "the cooking was atrocious."

Site of St. Mary's Pony Express Station,
west of the town of Sweetwater Station, Wyoming

Upper Sweetwater Station

Upper Sweetwater Station was ten miles east of the Continental Divide. At the divide, the Pony Express route followed the well-worn emigrant trail over South Pass. Because the trail's elevation rose so gradually, it was not a strenuous climb to here, the highest point on the route. But at this high altitude, the riders had to face frigid temperatures at night, even in the summer.

Rather than being narrow and confining like many mountain passes, South Pass is a virtually flat, treeless, sagebrush-covered plain nearly twenty miles wide. The only mountains visible from the pass are those in the Wind River Range, appearing blue and hazy to the north.

Trail near the site of Upper Sweetwater Pony Express Station, near South Pass City, Wyoming. The Wind River Mountains are in the background.

Pacific Springs Station

Pacific Springs Station, a small log shanty, was just two miles west of South Pass. Mosquitoes were a particular problem at this station. During the summer, the stationkeepers kept large smudge fires burning night and day to keep the pests away. In winter, bad storms were common, and riding through snowdrifts that could be as high as ten feet exhausted riders and their mounts.

*Buildings at Pacific Springs Pony Express Station,
west of South Pass City, Wyoming*

Dry Sandy Station

The stream near Dry Sandy Station was often dry, and when it did have water it was tainted with alkali and unfit for drinking. The stationkeeper, a young Mormon, and his wife obtained pure water by digging into the ground a distance away from the stream.

*Dry Sandy Creek near the site of Dry Sandy Pony Express Station,
northeast of Farson, Wyoming*

Stage road near Dry Sandy Station

Big Sandy Creek near the site of Big Sandy Pony Express Station, Farson, Wyoming

Big Sandy Station

Unlike Dry Sandy Station, Big Sandy Station had a plentiful supply of clear, cool water from Big Sandy Creek. An English couple, also Mormon, operated the station.

75

Green River Station

The Green River Pony Express and stage station was part of a relatively large settlement that spread out for about a mile along the bank of the Green River. In addition to the station, whose corrals contained a variety of livestock including sheep, horses, mules, and cows, the village had a grocery and several other stores. It also boasted a ferry, which was put into service during high waters. Fish from the river was often on the menu at the station.

Green River at the site of Green River Pony Express Station, southwest of Farson, Wyoming

Ham's Fork Station

Made of native rock, Ham's Fork Station was built as a stage station in 1850. David Lewis, a Scottish Mormon, managed the station along with his two wives and large family. It was a squalid, filthy place, full of flies. The furniture, such as it was, was cobbled together from parts of dilapidated wagons.

Buildings of the South Bend stage station, Granger, Wyoming;
Ham's Fork Pony Express Station was in a dugout nearby.

Church Buttes Station

Church Buttes, a sandstone formation rising seventy-five to one hundred feet in height, was another Oregon Trail landmark. Emigrants called it by that name because they thought it resembled a cathedral. The station was just west of the formation.

*Church Buttes at the Church Buttes Pony Express Station site,
north of Green River, Wyoming*

Fort Bridger Station

Mountain men Jim Bridger and Louis Vasquez established Fort Bridger in 1843 to service emigrants headed to Oregon and, later, to California and Salt Lake City. It was an ideal site, with abundant grass and game, on the Black's Fork River. In 1853, Brigham Young purchased the fort, replaced the original palisade structure with stone buildings, and added corrals. The place became an army post in 1858. The Pony Express picked up and delivered mail to the post office in the sutler's store. At Fort Bridger, the Oregon Trail turned north, while the Pony Express and stagecoach routes, as well as the Mormon Trail, bore southwest toward Salt Lake City.

Sutler's store, Fort Bridger State Historic Site, Fort Bridger, Wyoming

Pony Express stable at Fort Bridger State Historic Site

Thomas Owen King helped build many of the Pony Express stations east of Salt Lake City and subsequently became a rider between Fort Bridger and Salt Lake City. King was carrying the eastbound mail on the first Pony Express run in April 1860. Twenty miles from the fort, he encountered a bad storm. King's horse stumbled and threw him, and the mochila flew off the saddle and went over a cliff. King spent quite a bit of time climbing down to retrieve the mail. Once remounted, he urged his horse on. When he reached his destination he had made up the lost time and delivered the mail intact and on schedule.

On another occasion, after a night ride, King reported that he had not encountered his opposite rider, Henry Worley, on the way. When Worley pulled into his station, he reported the same thing—he had not seen King. The truth is, they did pass each other, but they were both asleep in the saddle. It was not uncommon for riders to sleep on their routes, trusting their horses to find the way.

5
❦ UTAH ❦
Stations and Stories

As soon as the Pony Express route left Wyoming, it entered Utah Territory and crossed the formidable Wasatch Mountains. Riders heading west faced numerous harrowing descents; exhausting climbs were in store for riders headed east. At the foot of the range, nearly three thousand feet below the summit, lay the valley of the Great Salt Lake.

Echo Canyon Station

Echo Canyon Station was in the Wasatch Mountains at the head of a deep long canyon. The canyon is about thirty miles long, and the broken and jagged red walls are as much as four hundred feet high in places. The Weber River, its banks lined with trees and grasses, runs through the narrow canyon, which is not more than three-quarters of a mile wide.

Mountain Dale Station

Ephraim Hanks, a Mormon and a relative of Abraham Lincoln, was the stationkeeper at Mountain Dale Station.

George Edwin Little, a fifteen-year-old Mormon boy, was a rider assigned to the route between Echo Canyon Station and Salt Lake City. One time when Little was on his way to Mountain Dale Station in a heavy snowstorm, his horse, exhausted from trying to forge its way through the deep drifts, finally gave out. Undeterred, Little used his pocketknife to cut open the cantinas, stuffed the mail inside his shirt, and plowed through the deep snow on foot, arriving at the station at three o'clock in the morning. As soon as it was light, he was off again on a fresh horse, carrying the mail to Salt Lake City.

Little, like so many other riders, had encounters with outlaws. On one occasion, two masked men ambushed him during a ride. He spurred his pony and rode off in a hail of gunfire, escaping unharmed.

Salt Lake City Station

Descending the mountains toward Salt Lake City Station, riders had a view of the thriving city below and beyond it the glimmering expanse of the Great Salt Lake. The Pony Express station was in Salt Lake House, a two-story, wood-frame structure with a long verandah—a far cry from the hovels and shanties of most other stations.

*Near the site of Mountain Dale Pony Express Station
in the Wasatch Mountains, east of Salt Lake City*

Camp Floyd Station

Camp Floyd Station was in Fairfield, Utah, a fairly large settlement with a population of 4,000 civilians and 3,000 soldiers garrisoned at Camp Floyd. The soldiers were the best customers of the town's seventeen saloons. After the Civil War started, Secretary of War John B. Floyd, for whom the fort was named, joined the Confederacy, and early in 1861 it was renamed Fort Crittenden. The Pony Express station was in Carson's Inn, operated by one of the town's founders, John Carson.

In a heavy snowstorm in 1860, on his regular westbound route from Salt Lake City to Rush Valley Station, rider Richard Erasmus Egan, son of division superintendent Howard Egan, stopped to change horses at Camp Floyd Station. It was sundown when he left the fort, and the snow was so deep that he could not see the road. Relying on the horse's instinct and keeping the wind on his right cheek, Egan rode all night. The next morning found him back at Camp Floyd—the wind direction had changed during the night and Egan had ridden in a circle. After changing horses he rode on to Rush Valley. Including the circular trip, he traveled an estimated 150 miles.

Egan made another notable long ride when a friend and fellow rider, William Fisher, wanted to get to Salt Lake City to see his girlfriend. On the way west, Egan met the eastbound Fisher at the station where they were to exchange mochilas and turn around. Instead, Fisher asked that Egan continue west, and Fisher would ride east to Salt Lake City. Egan had ridden 165 miles when he met the next eastbound rider and exchanged mochilas. He then turned around and rode back to Salt Lake City, for a total distance of 330 miles.

Carson's Inn, location of Camp Floyd Pony Express Station,
Camp Floyd and Stagecoach Inn State Park, Fairfield, Utah

*Vicinity of Lookout Pass near Point Lookout Pony Express Station,
west of American Fork, Utah*

Rush Valley Station

During the historic first run of the mail from Sacramento, Superintendent Howard Egan was on hand at Rush Valley Station. It was dark with sleet and blowing snow when the rider carrying the first eastbound mail arrived there. Egan decided to take the mail to Salt Lake City himself. On a plank bridge over a creek, Egan's horse lost its footing, and horse and rider plunged into the water. In just a few minutes, the soaked man and animal managed to get on the road again. Egan completed the ride almost on schedule.

Point Lookout Station

It was just a short distance west from the winding, rough, rocky trail through Lookout Pass to Point Lookout Station. From the pass, riders could gaze out over Skull Valley, a bleak and forbidding desert landscape that became known as "Paiute Hell" during the time of the Pony Express.

View of Skull Valley, also known as "Paiute Hell," west of Lookout Pass

Simpson's Springs Station

Unlike so many of the stations in desert areas, Simpson's Springs had an ample supply of good water from the nearby springs. The station and stable were built of native rock, and fine silt covered the surrounding land. Vegetation was sparse, mostly sagebrush and greasewood. The lack of trees made for dusty conditions when the wind blew—which was most of the time.

Restored Simpson's Springs Pony Express Station
on Pony Express Byway, west of Faust, Utah

*Stagecoach road at Black Rock Pony Express Station
on Pony Express Byway, west of Faust, Utah*

Black Rock Station

Black Rock Station was constructed of rock from the large volcanic outcrop nearby.

Volcanic outcrop from which Black Rock Station was built

Boyd's Station

Boyd's Station was named for Bid Boyd, the stationkeeper. It was built of stone collected from the surrounding countryside. For defense against Indians, the building had several gun ports. Here the trail diverted from the old Chorpenning route it had been following and went straight west.

Ruins of Boyd's Pony Express Station on Pony Express Byway, west of Faust, Utah

Willow Creek Station

Rider Elijah Nichols "Uncle Nick" Wilson had many run-ins with the Paiute Indians, one of which occurred at Willow Creek Station. One afternoon, seven Paiutes from a nearby encampment of about thirty warriors rode up and asked the stationkeeper, Peter Neece, for something to eat. Neece gave them a twenty-pound bag of flour, but the Indians demanded a bag apiece, so Neece threw the bag back inside the station and told them he would not give them anything.

Although the Paiutes rode off, Neece was sure there would be trouble that night, so he and the three other men at the station, including the fifteen-year-old Wilson, prepared a defense. The men took their weapons and hid in the brush outside the station. Because it was dark, Neece figured the Indians would aim at the flash of the guns, so he instructed the others to jump to the side after they fired.

The Indians did indeed attack that night. When Wilson heard the noise of the galloping horses' hooves and the warriors' blood-curdling yells, although he had two pistols cocked and ready, he didn't fire. But jumping after every shot fired by the other men, he landed in a small ravine. Crouching there, he waited for about two hours until all was still. Finally, thinking the others were dead, he crept back to the station. Peering through a chink in the logs, he saw all three of them alive and well. Later he found out that the men had been searching for him, assuming he had run off to chase the Indians by himself.

98

Ravine near the site of Willow Creek Pony Express Station, north of Callao, Utah

Canyon Station

In another close call with Paiutes, "Uncle Nick" Wilson was on his way through Overland Canyon, the canyon for which Canyon Station was named, when four Indians jumped from the rocks and surrounded him, taking his revolver and his horse. The leader of the group told Wilson that this was their land and he had no right to cross it. Then Wilson recognized one of the Indians, a man called Tabby, a friend of his father. Tabby showed no sign that he knew Wilson, however.

The warriors moved away a short distance and began to argue among themselves. One came back and asked Wilson for some tobacco. He handed it over, and the Indians sat smoking for a while. Eventually Tabby approached Wilson and told him that although the others wanted to kill him, Tabby had persuaded them to let him go, as long as he promised never to ride over their land again. Wilson agreed, on the condition that they give him back the mail. The Indians returned Wilson's horse with the mochila. Wilson was able to keep his promise because he was assigned to another route soon afterward.

Overland Canyon east of Canyon Pony Express Station, north of Callao, Utah

Stage road across Antelope Valley near
Antelope Springs Pony Express Station, south of Tippet, Nevada

6

❋ NEVADA ❋
Stations and Stories

INDIAN RESENTMENT of the white man's intrusion west of the Great Salt Lake heightened during the 1840s and 1850s, when thousands of gold seekers and emigrants crossed these lands on their way to California. Some even settled in Nevada Territory on lands that treaties had supposedly guaranteed to the Paiutes. The Indians began to wage frequent attacks against the whites, and the whites retaliated in kind, leading to years of unrest and conflict.

The situation was coming to a head in the spring of 1860, when the Paiutes held a council at Pyramid Lake to discuss what to do. Some white men at William's Stage Station in western Nevada had recently taken two Indian women captive, and one chief, Mogoannoga, impatient with the council proceedings, stole away one night with a band of warriors to raid the station. The Indians burned the station, killed

five men, and rescued the women. After the raid, a volunteer corps of area settlers and miners marched to Pyramid Lake in an attempted retaliation but were soundly defeated.

By May 1860 the Paiutes and the settlers were engaged in all-out war. Because of the hostilities, on May 21, just a little over a month after the first ride, the Pony Express service came to a temporary halt as personnel manning stations over a 250-mile length prepared to defend themselves. In June the government sent in troops, and Bolivar Roberts, the division superintendent based in Carson City, led a party of riders, stationkeepers, and stock tenders to rebuild destroyed stations. After constructing them to withstand attacks better, Roberts left five men to stay at each station until the Indian troubles were over.

The mail service resumed, but small-scale Indian raids continued for over a year. Before the war was over, seven stations had been burned; 150 horses had been killed, stolen, or run off; and sixteen station personnel had been killed. Although the riders feared for their lives every time they set out, not one was killed during a run.

Antelope Springs Station

Antelope Springs Station was built as a stage station in 1859. During the Paiute War, Indians attacked it and burned all the buildings.

Spring Valley Station

Spring Valley Station was the site of another Indian encounter for "Uncle Nick" Wilson. One evening the two stock tenders at the station invited him to stay for dinner. While the men were eating, they looked up and saw two Indians driving off their horses. The men chased them on foot, Wilson firing his revolver as he ran. Suddenly an arrow struck Wilson in the forehead about two inches above his left eye. The stock tenders rushed to help him. When they tugged on the arrow, the shaft came loose but the arrowhead remained imbedded in his skull. The injured man's two companions left him under a tree and ran to the next station for help, though they assumed he would soon die.

When the men came back they were prepared to bury Wilson, but he wasn't dead—just unconscious. A doctor came the next day and removed the arrowhead, but he doubted that Wilson would live. He did recover, however, and several weeks later he was riding for the Pony Express again. For the rest of his life Wilson suffered from severe headaches and never removed his hat in public.

Ruins of Antelope Springs Station

Stage road near Schell Creek Pony Express Station, north of Ely, Nevada

Schell Creek Station

When Sir Richard Burton stopped at Schell Creek Station, the Paiute War had been over for months, yet there was still evidence of the fighting. He noted, "This log hut . . . showed the bullet marks of a recent Indian attack." The Indians had indeed attacked the station—they killed the stationkeeper and his two assistants and ran off all the livestock.

Looking west down the stagecoach road that leads to the mouth of Egan's Canyon, north of Ely, Nevada

Egan's Canyon

Narrow Egan's Canyon was an ideal spot for Indian ambushes. One night, as rider Howard Ransom Egan, another son of the division superintendent, was riding west through Egan's Canyon, he spotted some Indians clustered around a campfire and pondered what to do. One choice would be to detour through another canyon to the north, but he suspected there might be Indians there too. He decided that the best approach was a direct one, so, yelling and firing his revolver, he charged directly at the Indians. Thinking a large party of whites was attacking, they scattered in all directions. Egan reached the station safely.

Later, a friendly Indian told Egan that the war party in the canyon had been waiting to catch a Pony Express rider. They wanted to find out what he carried that made him ride so fast.

Egan's Canyon east of Egan's Canyon Pony Express Station

Site of Egan's Canyon Station

Egan's Canyon Station

Egan's Canyon Station was in a meadow at the west end of the canyon from which it got its name, and like the canyon, the station was the site of several Indian incursions. In July 1860, stationkeeper Mike Holton and rider Henry Woodville "Slim" Wilson were having breakfast when a war party of thirty Paiutes swooped down on the station. The men grabbed their guns and started firing. Although the Indians had no guns, they managed to break through the station door just as Holton and Wilson ran out of bullets. The chief asked for bread, and Holton piled all the bread he had on the table. This didn't satisfy the chief. He pointed at some sacks of flour and indicated that they bake more.

All day long Holton and Wilson baked bread and fed the Indians. They feared that rider William Dennis, due in that afternoon, would be captured when he arrived, and when Dennis didn't show up, they assumed the Paiutes had killed him. At sunset the flour ran out. The chief ordered the two men to be taken outside and tied up. The Indians piled sagebrush around the men's feet and set it on fire, then began to yell and dance around the terrified men.

As it happened, Dennis was alive, but late. As he neared the station, he saw what the Indians were up to. He turned around and sped five miles back to where he had passed a detachment of sixty dragoons. Soon the dragoons charged into the station, killed eighteen Indians, and freed Holton and Wilson, who were uninjured. Three soldiers were killed in the action; some say they are buried in the cemetery at the station.

Cemetery at Egan's Canyon Station

View of Ruby Valley, Nevada

Ruby Valley Station

The land surrounding Ruby Valley Station had rich soil, so after the station was built, the Pony Express established a farm here to supply food and hay for other stations along the route. The army maintained troops there during the Paiute War, from June to October 1860.

Ruby Valley Station was the only station for miles around that the Paiutes did not attack. The reason it escaped that fate may have been that Colonel William "Uncle Billy" Rogers, the stationkeeper and assistant Indian agent, was especially friendly to the Indians. He had fed them during the brutal winter of 1859-60 and tried to teach them how to grow their own food.

Ruby Valley Pony Express Station, relocated to Elko, Nevada

Diamond Springs Station

William Cox was the stationkeeper at Diamond Springs Station. Like so many other stationkeepers in Utah and Nevada, he was a Mormon. The station was named for its spring, the "diamond" probably referring to the small, glittering quartz crystals in the soil.

The one-room station was built of slabs of limestone held together with mud, with a roof of split cedar logs covered with dirt. The gables and part of the chimney were made of adobe. During the Paiute War, Diamond Springs served as a gathering spot for riders and stationkeepers waiting for troops to arrive.

*Ruins of Diamond Springs Pony Express Station,
north of Eureka, Nevada*

Roberts Creek Station

Shortly after Roberts Creek Station was built in April 1860, Paiutes drove off the horses, delaying the mail for six hours. The next month, Indians burned the station. The Pony Express rebuilt it in June.

Stagecoach road east of Roberts Creek Pony Express Station, north of Eureka, Nevada

Dry Creek Station

Like so many other stations in the area, Dry Creek Station had its share of Indian problems. In one incident, Pauites killed stationkeeper Ralph Rosier outside the cabin. His assistant John Applegate rushed to the door to see what had happened and was shot in the hip. The other station assistant, Lafayette "Bolly" Bolwinkle, jumped out of bed, and trading-post operator Si McCandless came dashing over from across the road.

Applegate urged the other men to leave him and try to get away, but they refused.

When he asked for a revolver, his companions, thinking he was going to continue the fight, gave him one. But Applegate, knowing he was going to die anyway, shot himself in the head. Then McCandless and Bolwinkle decided to make a break for it. As they ran down the road, a few Indians chased them on foot, but they soon gave up and went back to loot the station. The men arrived safely at the next station, Bolwinkle suffering from cuts on his feet. He had neglected to put on his boots and had made the twelve-mile run in his stocking feet.

Ruins of Dry Creek Pony Express Station, east of Austin, Nevada

Reese River near Reese River Pony Express Station, west of Austin, Nevada

Reese River Station

The Indians burned Reese River Station in May 1860, but it was rebuilt of adobe a few months later. The station was about two miles east of the Reese River.

122

Ruins of Cold Springs Pony Express Station in the distance, east of Fallon, Nevada

Cold Springs Station

Many riders thought Cold Springs Station was an unlucky place because it was attacked so many times. Even though it was larger than many of the other stations and sturdily built, with a guard posted day and night, the Paiutes managed to get through. The stone structure measured 110 feet by 50 feet. It was divided into four rooms and had walls two feet thick. The corral abutted the building. In May 1860, Indians killed the station-keeper, John Williams, and ran off the horses. A few weeks later, they raided the station again.

123

East of Cold Springs Station was a part of the trail that was especially dangerous. It was a two-mile-long section in an area called Quaking Aspen Bottom. Heavily wooded and so narrow that there was room for only the horse and rider, the place was ideal for an ambush. On one occasion, the assistant stationkeeper at Cold Springs Station, J. G. Kelley, took over for a rider who had been shot by Paiutes as he rode through Quaking Aspen Bottom. Passing through on the return route, Kelley sensed that Indians were lurking about. He dropped the reins, put his rifle at full cock, spurred his horse, and went through "like a streak of greased lightning," as he later described it. When he stopped to let his horse rest at the top of a hill, he looked back and noticed movement in the bushes and fired several shots into them. The movement ceased. He knew then that Indians had indeed been waiting for him. Several days later, two soldiers on their way to rejoin their command were killed at Quaking Aspen Bottom.

Gun port at Cold Springs Station

Ruins of Cold Springs Station

Ruins of Sand Springs Pony Express Station, east of Fallon, Nevada

Sand Springs Station

Sand Springs Station was in an area of sand dunes, some as high as two hundred feet. Sir Richard Burton described the place: "The water near this vile hole was thick and stale with sulphury salts: it blistered even the hands. The station-house was . . . roofless and chairless, filthy and squalid, with a smoky fire in one corner, and a table in the centre of an impure floor, the walls open to every wind, and the interior full of dust."

During the Paiute War, Indians kept up a continual harassment of the station, but none came near enough to be shot by the round-the-clock guards.

Sand dune with ruins of Sand Springs Station in the foreground

Carson Sink Station

When Carson Sink Station was a stage stop, it was nothing more than several rude brush shelters, as there were no rocks or logs in the vicinity. When the Pony Express took it over, employees constructed a more substantial station of adobe, made of mud from adjacent Lake Carson. The men worked the mud with their bare feet. Because it was extremely alkaline, the men ended up with feet so swollen that one worker remarked that they resembled hams.

Vicinity of Carson Sink Pony Express Station, south of Fallon, Nevada

Buckland's Station

Buckland's Station was established on the ranch of Samuel S. Buckland. During the Paiute War, the Pony Express moved its station about a mile west to Fort Churchill, which was still under construction. The company continued to use the stable and corrals at Buckland's.

Stable and corrals at Buckland's Pony Express Station, southwest of Fallon, Nevada; ruins of Fort Churchill in the background

Post headquarters building in which the Fort Churchill Pony Express station was located, Fort Churchill State Historic Park, southwest of Fallon, Nevada

Fort Churchill Station

The Paiute War precipitated the construction of Fort Churchill, a large facility covering 1,384 acres on the north side of the Carson River. The fort's buildings, constructed of adobe on stone foundations, were arranged in a square, facing a parade ground in the center. The headquarters building served as the Pony Express office.

Ruins of Fort Churchill, Fort Churchill State Historic Park

Carson City Station

The Pony Express station in Carson City was the base of division superintendent Bolivar Roberts. Carson City was a relative metropolis, boasting a population of twelve hundred people, between many miles of desolate desert to the east and the imposing Sierra Nevada to the west.

Genoa Station

Genoa Pony Express Station lay at the foot of the eastern slopes of the Sierra Nevada. The first building in the settlement of Genoa was Mormon Station, a log cabin surrounded by a stockade. The Pony Express station was in the post office across the street, and the stable was next to the stockade.

Mormon Station State Historic Park, across the street from the Pony Express station, Genoa, Nevada

Kingsbury Grade Road

The Kingsbury Grade Road was a new wagon road that led over the Sierra Nevada. For the Pony Express horses, it was an exhausting climb, the steepest one on the entire route. In about ten miles, the road rose more than 2,500 feet up to Daggett Pass, 7,334 feet above sea level.

Pony Express route on Kingsbury Grade Road, east of Daggett Pass, Nevada

Friday's Station

Friday's Station, near the California border, was the home station of rider Robert "Pony Bob" Haslam. Haslam had several narrow escapes from Indians and was wounded twice.

On May 9, 1860, unaware that an all-out war was in progress, Haslam set out on his usual eastbound route from Friday's Station to Buckland's Station. In Carson City he learned about recent Indian attacks, and when he reached Miller's Station, the first station west of Fort Churchill, he found that volunteers had taken all the horses to fight the Paiutes and there was no fresh mount for him.

On his exhausted horse, he rode on to Buckland's and reported what he had learned. Hearing this, Johnson Richardson, the rider scheduled to take the next leg, refused to go. The stationkeeper, W. C. Marley, offered Haslam fifty dollars to continue the ride. Haslam, having already ridden seventy-five miles, agreed to go—not because of the bonus, but because it was his duty.

In less than ten minutes, Haslam was on his way again. He rode the thirty-five miles to Carson Sink Station without changing mounts. From there, he rode thirty miles to Sand Springs Station, changed mounts, and went on to Cold Springs Station, a distance of thirty-seven miles. His next stop was Smith Creek, thirty miles away, where another rider finally took over. Haslam had covered 190 miles without a rest.

Haslam remained at Smith Creek Station for about nine hours, then was off again with the westbound mail. When he reached Cold Springs Station, he found that Paiutes had killed the stationkeeper and driven away all the horses. He fed and watered his horse and went on. Riding in the dark, he finally managed to reach Buckland's Station, only three and a half hours behind schedule.

As a reward, stationkeeper Marley boosted his bonus to one hundred dollars. Haslam rested for about ninety minutes before riding to Friday's Station to complete his route. In the thirty-six hours he had spent in the saddle, he had ridden a total of 380 miles. (See Appendix B, Robert "Pony Bob" Haslam.)

The Pony Express Trail immediately west of Friday's Station, Stateline, Nevada

Echo Summit area, east of Strawberry
Pony Express Station, Strawberry, California

7
❧ CALIFORNIA ❧
Stations and Stories

IN CALIFORNIA, which had achieved statehood in 1850, many miles of the Pony Express route were in the lofty Sierra Nevada. Due to the steep and rugged terrain, the going was rough enough in good weather, but in winter riders had to endure the cold and travel through deep snow as well. Yet day and night, in all seasons, they pushed through and rarely failed to deliver the mail on time.

Yank's Station

Yank's Station was a hostelry and stage station before the Pony Express added a relay station there. After Ephraim "Yank" Clement and his wife, Lydia, purchased the place in 1859, they made many improvements. These included enlarging the hostelry to a three-story structure containing fourteen guest rooms and adding a large barn and corrals.

Strawberry Station

Strawberry Station was the first station west of Echo Summit, the highest point on the Pony Express route through the Sierra Nevada. Like Yank's Station, it was already a hostelry when the Pony Express established a station there. A Mr. Berry managed the place, which reputedly got its name because Berry was known to feed travelers' horses straw instead of the higher-priced hay for which their owners had paid.

Mountain behind Strawberry Station site

Sportsman's Hall Station

Sportsman's Hall Station was the first home station east of Sacramento. On the first Pony Express run, Warren "Boston" Upson, son of the editor of the *Sacramento Union,* was ready and waiting early in the morning when rider Sam Hamilton came galloping in from Sacramento. The riders switched the mochila in two minutes and Upson set off over the Sierra Nevada summit. It would not be an easy ride because heavy snow had obliterated the trail.

At Strawberry Station, Bolivar Roberts was waiting for Upson with a string of mules to help break the trail to Echo Summit. Even so, Upson often had to lead his horse through the snow on foot. Despite the difficulty, he arrived in Carson City late but safe. Many had expected that he wouldn't make it all.

Placerville Station

Placerville Station was a relay station until July 1, 1861, when the telegraph reached the town and Placerville became the westernmost Pony Express station. It was at the junction of White Rock and Green Valley Roads, both of which were used by the Pony Express at different times. (See Appendix A for a listing of stations on the two routes.)

Mormon Tavern Station

For riders heading west, Mormon Tavern was the second station on the White Rock Road. The Pony Express used this road until the route was changed to follow the Green Valley Road in July 1860.

Approximate site of Mormon Tavern Pony Express Station,
on White Rock Road near Clarksville, California

Pleasant Grove House Station

Pleasant Grove House Station, on the Green Valley Road, was built as an inn in 1850. It became a Pony Express station after the route change in July 1860. (See Appendix A.)

Pleasant Grove House Pony Express Station, north of Rescue, California

Folsom Station

Folsom Station became the western terminus of the Pony Express after July 1, 1860, when the Sacramento Valley Railroad began carrying express mail between Folsom and Sacramento.

An interesting incident happened one day before the railroad took over the mail delivery. A Pony Express rider on his way from Folsom to Sacramento was thrown from his horse just as a Wells Fargo stage passed him. The stage driver halted to aid the rider, who had broken his leg. J. G. McCall, a special agent for Wells Fargo and a passenger on the stage, volunteered to finish the ride into Sacramento for the injured rider. McCall arrived an hour and a half late, but thanks to him, the mail went through.

*Wells Fargo Building, location of the Folsom
Pony Express Station, Folsom, California*

The Hastings Building, in which the Wells Fargo office and Sacramento Pony Express Station were located, Sacramento, California

Sacramento Station

The Alta Telegraph Company housed the first Sacramento Pony Express station, but it was later moved to the Wells Fargo Company office. Mail destined for San Francisco, usually the bulk of the west-bound mail, came from Sacramento by steamboat down the Sacramento River. If the westbound rider was late and missed the connection with the boat, he had to go overland to Oakland and then by ferry to San Francisco.

Sacramento Pony Express Station at the Wells Fargo office

8
✖ THE SHORT, USEFUL LIFE ✖
of the Pony Express

THE MOTTO OF THE PONY EXPRESS was "the mail must go through," and go through it did, sometimes bettering its scheduled ten-day delivery from St. Joseph to San Francisco. But no matter how fast it was, everyone knew from the outset that it was only a temporary service eventually to be replaced by the telegraph.

Before the Pony Express came into existence, telegraph lines already reached from the East Coast to cities along the Missouri River, and some telegraph service existed in California and Nevada. It was only matter of time before the lines reached across the country. The time proved to be short, for on June 16, 1860, Congress passed a bill subsidizing the building of a transcontinental telegraph line. Just eighteen days later, on July 4, the Overland Telegraph Company of California started building from the west, and workmen began stringing the line of the Pacific

Telegraph Company of Nebraska in the Midwest. The lines, spanning a combined distance of fifteen hundred miles, would join at Salt Lake City. As the lines advanced, Pony Express riders continued to carry mail from St. Joseph to Sacramento, as well as telegrams between the ever-advancing eastern and western telegraph terminals.

The transcontinental telegraph line was completed on October 24, 1861, effectively putting the Pony Express out of business—a mere nineteen months after it started. No longer was there a need for speedy mail delivery when the telegraph could deliver news and messages in hours.

During its short life, the Pony Express was a money-losing proposition. The first western run netted the company only $260, and the first eastward run, just $425. With the maximum weight limit set at twenty pounds, the best the company could hope to earn from any single trip would be $3,200—hardly enough to pay the riders and station personnel and to buy supplies. No trip ever brought in close to that amount. The most the company ever made from a trip was a mere $1,000, and that happened only once.

The final tally for operating the Pony Express was: $100,000 for equipping the line; $480,000 for maintenance; $75,000 for repairing ruined property, replacing stolen goods and horses, and purchasing military supplies due to the Paiute Indian War; and $45,000 in miscellaneous expenditures. The total came to $700,000, yet the receipts were only $500,000, netting a loss of $200,000.

Although short-lived, the Pony Express captured the fancy of those living during the time of its existence and continues to fascinate us even today. The dashing, intrepid riders, carrying the mail night and day no matter what the weather, through barren stretches of alkali and sage, across mountain ranges, in desert heat and in frigid winters, through torrential rain and deep snow drifts, and in spite of danger from outlaws and hostile Indians, remain a symbol of the daring vision and bold entrepreneurial spirit that shaped our country.

❋ APPENDIX A ❋
The Stations

STATIONS WENT IN AND OUT of service during the life of the Pony Express, so the total number differed from time to time. We identify 160 Pony Express stations, but other sources may disagree and put the total either higher or lower.

A station may have had several names. In the following list, the most common name is noted first, followed by any other names sometimes used. Again, some sources may disagree with our determina-tion of the most common name. Note that some stations in one state may have the same names as stations in a different state.

The stations are listed from east to west. The number preceding the name of each station is not any official Pony Express designation; they are only to show the order of the stations. Those without a number weren't official Pony Express sta-tions but were used as stops for pickup and delivery of mail.

Missouri
1. St. Joseph Station

Kansas
— Elwood
2. Troy Station
3. Lewis Station (Cold Springs)
4. Kennekuk Station
5. Goteschall Station (Kickapoo)
6. Log Chain Station
7. Seneca Station
8. Ash Point Station
   (Laramie Creek, Hickory Point)
9. Guittard's Station
   (Vermillion Creek)
10. Marysville Station
    (Big Blue, Palmetto City)
11. Cottonwood Station (Hollenberg's)

Nebraska

12. Rock House Station
    (Otoe, Caldwell)
13. Rock Creek Station
    (Pawnee, Turkey Creek)
14. Virginia City Station (Grayson's)
15. Big Sandy Station
16. Millersville Station (Thompson's)
17. Kiowa Station
18. Little Blue Station (Oak Grove)
19. Liberty Farm Station
20. Spring Ranch Station
    (Lone Tree)
21. Thirty-two Mile Creek Station
22. Summit Station
    (Sand Hill, Water Hole,
    Fairfield)
23. Kearny Station
    (Hook's Ranch, Valley,
    Dogtown)
—— Fort Kearny
24. Platte's Station (Seventeen Mile)
25. Craig's Station (Garden)
26. Plum Creek Station
27. Willow Island Station
    (Willow Bend)
28. Midway Station
    (Cold Water Ranch)
29. Gilman's Station
30. Machette's Station*
31. Cottonwood Springs Station
    (McDonald's Ranch)
32. Cold Springs Station (Box Elder)
33. Fremont Springs Station
34. O'Fallon's Bluff Station
    (Dansey's, Elkhorn Station)

35. Alkali Lake Station (Pike's Peak)
36. Gill's Station (Sand Hill)
37. Diamond Springs Station

Colorado

38. Frontz's Station (South Platte)
39. Julesburg Station

Nebraska

40. Nine Mile Station
41. Pole Creek No. 2 Station
42. Pole Creek No. 3 Station
    (Lodgepole)
43. Unnamed (May have been called
    Midway Station at some time)
44. Mud Springs Station
45. Courthouse Rock Station
46. Chimney Rock Station
47. Ficklin's Springs Station
48. Scott's Bluff Station
    (Fort Mitchell)
49. Horse Creek Station

Wyoming

50. Cold Springs Station
    (Spring Ranch, Torrington)
51. Verdling's Ranch Station
    (Bordeaux, Bedeau's Ranch,
    Beauvais's Ranch)
52. Fort Laramie Station
53. Ward's Station
    (Sand Point, Nine Mile,
    Central Star)
54. Cottonwood Station
55. Horseshoe Creek Station
56. Elk Horn Station
57. La Bonte Station

* Machette's may not have been a Pony Express station, although according to some sources it was. The main argument against its being a station is that it was too close to adjacent stations— Cottonwood Springs was five miles to the west, and Gilman's, seven and a half miles to the east. Given how Pony Express stations were usually positioned, it seems unlikely that there would have been a station between Cottonwood Springs and Gilman's. Machette's was a stage line relay and repair station with a blacksmith shop, so its facilities may have been used by the Pony Express.

58. Bed Tick Station
59. La Prele Station
60. Boxelder Creek Station
61. Deer Creek Station
62. Little Muddy Station (Bridger)
63. Platte Bridge Station
    (North Platte)
64. Red Buttes Station
65. Willow Springs Station
66. Horse Creek Station
    (Greasewood Creek)
67. Sweetwater Station
68. Plant's Station (Plante)
69. Split Rock Station
70. Three Crossings Station
71. Ice Slough Station (Ice Springs)
72. Warm Springs Station
73. St. Mary's Station (Rocky Ridge)
74. Rock Creek Station (Strawberry)
75. Upper Sweetwater Station
    (South Pass, Burnt Ranch,
    Gilbert's)
76. Pacific Springs Station
77. Dry Sandy Station
78. Little Sandy Creek Station
79. Big Sandy Station (Farson)
80. Big Timber Station (Big Bend)
81. Green River Station
    (Green River Crossing)
82. Michael Martin's Station
83. Ham's Fork Station
    (Granger, South Bend
    Stage Station)
84. Church Buttes Station
85. Millersville Station
86. Fort Bridger Station
87. Muddy Creek Station
88. Quaking Aspen Station (Springs)
89. Bear River Station (Briggs)

Utah

90. Needles Station (Needle Rock)
91. Echo Canyon Station
    (Castle Rock, Frenchie's)
92. Halfway Station (Daniel's, Emory)
93. Weber Station
    (Bromley's, Echo, Hanging Rock)
94. Carson House Station
95. East Canyon Station
    (Dixie Creek, Snyder's Mill,
    Baughmann's)
96. Wheaton Springs Station
    (Winston Springs)
97. Mountain Dale Station
    (Mountain Dell,
    Big Canyon, Hank's)
98. Salt Lake City Station
99. Trader's Rest Station
    (Traveler's Rest)
100. Rockwell's Station
101. Dugout Station (Joe's Dugout)
102. Camp Floyd Station
    (Carson's Inn, Fort
    Crittenden, Fairfield)
103. Pass Station
    (East Rush Valley,
    Five Mile Pass)
104. Rush Valley Station
    (Faust's, Meadow Creek)
105. Point Lookout Station
    (Lookout Pass)
106. Government Creek Station
    (Davis, Government Well)
107. Simpson's Springs Station
    (Pleasant Springs,
    Egan's Springs)
108. River Bed Station
109. Dugway Station (Dugout)

110. Black Rock Station
     (Butte, Desert)
111. Fish Springs Station
     (Smith Springs)
112. Boyd's Station
113. Willow Springs Station
114. Willow Creek Station
115. Canyon Station (Burnt)
116. Deep Creek Station (Egan's)

Nevada
117. Prairie Gate Station (Eight Mile)
118. Antelope Springs Station
119. Spring Valley Station
120. Schell Creek Station
121. Egan's Canyon Station
122. Butte Station
     (Bate's, Robbers' Roost)
123. Mountain Springs Station
124. Ruby Valley Station
125. Jacob's Well Station
126. Diamond Springs Station
127. Sulphur Springs Station
128. Roberts Creek Station
129. Grubb's Well Station (Camp)
130. Dry Creek Station
131. Simpson Park Station
132. Reese River Station
     (Jacob's Spring)
133. Dry Wells Station
134. Smith's Creek Station
135. Cold Springs Station (East Gate)
136. Middle Gate Station
137. Sand Springs Station

138. Sand Hill Station
139. Carson Sink Station
     (Sink of the Carson)
140. Buckland's Station
141. Fort Churchill Station
142. Miller's Station (Reed's)
143. Dayton Station
144. Carson City Station
145. Genoa Station
146. Friday's Station (Lakeside)

California
147. Woodford's Station
148. Yank's Station
149. Strawberry Station
150. Webster's Station
     (Sugar Loaf House)
151. Moss Station (Moore, Riverton)
152. Sportsman's Hall Station
153. Placerville Station*

White Rock Road Route
154. El Dorado Station
     (Nevada House, Mud Springs)
155. Mormon Tavern Station
     (Sunrise House)
156. Fifteen Mile House Station

Green Valley Road Route
157. Pleasant Grove House Station**
158. Folsom Station
159. Five Mile House Station
     (Magnolia House)
160. Sacramento Station

*   Placerville Station was the eastern junction of both the White Rock Road (in use until June 1860) and the Green Valley Road (used thereafter); Five Mile House Station was the western junction.

** Some sources list Pleasant Grove House as only a stage station, yet other sources list it as also a Pony Express station.

❧ APPENDIX B ❧
Legends of the Pony Express:
Facts and Fictions

SOME HISTORIANS HAVE CHALLENGED certain accounts of events that occurred during the days of the Pony Express as being inaccurate, exaggerated, or even false-hoods. In the retelling of events, the truth was often manipulated to make the story more exciting and the hero—often the storyteller himself—braver, stronger, or more fearless than he actually was. For ex-ample, if someone shot a deer, in the subsequent story the deer might turn into a big bear—if the storyteller thought he could get away with it. Furthermore, it was common for nineteenth-century journalists and authors, upon hearing these stories, to add their own embellish-ments and perhaps turn a dastardly deed into an act of bravery, or make a rather bland story into something lurid or blood-curdling. The result has been distorted history and the perpetuation of inaccu-rate legends.

In researching the people involved with the Pony Express, we sifted through dif-fering versions of their stories to find which facts most sources agreed on and what seemed most plausible to us. Below are our brief comments on some of the most controversial figures.

The First Westbound Rider

Many sources, some of them eye-witnesses to the event, maintain that the first westbound rider from St. Joseph was either John Frye or Billy Richardson. When the identity of the first rider was in dispute, a person named Billy Richardson came forward claiming to have been the first rider. He later denied it after someone found records proving he was only twelve years old at the time of the first ride. Records showed that there was a second person named William "Billy" Richardson who rode for the Pony

Express, and most historians now believe it was this Richardson who made the famous ride.

The Longest Ride and Other Claims

It was a point of pride with some Pony Express riders to claim that they made the longest or the fastest rides. There are virtually no records to verify their claims, and to give the riders the benefit of the doubt, some of them probably made honest mistakes in estimating the number of miles they rode since there was no accurate way to measure distance in those days. One of those riders claiming to have made the longest ride was "Buffalo Bill" Cody.

William Frederick "Buffalo Bill" Cody

William Cody, later better known as Buffalo Bill, was one whose stories, whether true or not, were related repeatedly in publications of the day that tried to capitalize on his name. Eventually so much was written that it became difficult to determine what was the writer's imagination, what was Cody's own embellishment, and what was the truth.

One of Cody's claims is that he made the longest ride and he may have; that is, if he was truly a Pony Express rider. Some sources maintain that at fifteen years of age, Cody was too young to have ridden for the Pony Express. However, a number of riders were his age or younger. Several were fifteen, two were fourteen, and one rider claimed to be only thirteen. Qualified riders were not plentiful, particularly in the western portion of the route, so the company took them where they could find them. In her memoirs, Cody's older sister, Julia, states that young Will was in school during the period in which he claims to have ridden for the Pony Express. But his younger sister, Helen, claims in her biography of his life that he was a Pony Express rider and did make the longest ride.

One fact on which most sources agree is that Cody worked for Alexander Majors as a messenger on a wagon train before the Pony Express days, so he may well have continued in Majors's employ as a rider. In later years, Majors did not refute Cody's claims. In fact, Majors thought so much of him that he had Cody write the preface to his autobiography. Or was Majors perhaps engaging in his own bit of exploitation of Cody's name?

Robert "Pony Bob" Haslam

"Pony Bob" Haslam was another famous Pony Express rider. Haslam supposedly made a long and heroic ride during the Paiute War. Many sources, including Majors's autobiography, describe his ride. Yet some sources claim that he never rode for the Pony Express, and that an unknown rider made the run and Haslam simply took credit for it. Certain sources list him as a driver for the stage line, but not as a rider.

James Butler
"Wild Bill" Hickok

"Wild Bill" Hickok was not a rider but a stable hand for the Pony Express. There is no doubt that Hickok shot David McCanles at Rock Creek Station. The story as we have related it is true according to the research materials we used. Had we relied only on an article by Colonel Ward Nichols in the February 1867 issue of *Harper's Weekly* magazine for an account, we would have painted a much different picture. Ward glorified Hickok as a hero who saved the Pony Express station single-handedly, armed with only a gun and a bowie knife. With these weapons, he killed ten men—the "M'Kandlas's Gang . . . reckless, blood-thirsty devils who would fight as long as they had strength to pull a trigger." Ward went on to say that Hickok, even with eleven buckshot and thirteen knife wounds, managed to dispatch the gang. So Hickok became a legend for his heroism, instead of being vilified for the cold-blooded murders of McCanles and his two employees.

❈ BIBLIOGRAPHY ❈

Bensen, Joe. *Traveler's Guide to the Pony Express Trail*. Helena, Mont.: Falcon Press, 1995.

Blake, Herbert Cody. *Blake's Western Stories*. Brooklyn: Herbert Cody Blake, 1929.

Bloss, Roy S. *Pony Express: The Great Gamble*. Berkeley: Howell-North Press, 1959.

Bureau of Land Management, "The Pony Express in Nevada." *Pamphlet*, n.d.

Burke, John M. *"Buffalo Bill" from Prairie to Palace*. New York: Rand, McNally & Co., 1893.

Burton, Sir Richard F. *The City of the Saints*. 1862. Reprint. Niwot, Colo.: University Press of Colorado, 1990.

Carter, Kate B. *Riders of the Pony Express*. Salt Lake City: Daughters of Utah Pioneers, 1947.

Chapman, Arthur. *The Pony Express*. New York: G. P. Putnam's Sons, 1932.

Di Certo, Joseph J. *The Saga of the Pony Express*. Missoula, Mont.: Mountain Press, 2002.

Driggs, Howard R. *The Pony Express Goes Through*. New York: J. B. Lippincott Co., 1935.

Fike, Richard E., and John W. Headley. *Pony Express Stations of Utah in Historical Perspective*. Washington, D.C.: Bureau of Land Management, 1979.

Floyd, William H. *Phantom Riders of the Pony Express*. Philadelphia: Dorrance & Co., 1958.

Franzwa, Gregory M. *Maps of the California Trail*. Tucson: Patrice Press, 1999.

———. *Maps of the Oregon Trail*. Gerald, Mo: Patrice Press, 1982.

———. *The Oregon Trail Revisited*. Tucson: Patrice Press, 1997.

Godfrey, Anthony. *Historic Resource Study, Pony Express National Historic Trail*. Washington, D.C.: United States Department of the Interior/National Park Service, 1994.

Gray, John S. "Fact versus Fiction in the Kansas Boyhood of Buffalo Bill." *Kansas History* 8, no. 1 (Spring 1985).

Hafen, LeRoy R. *The Overland Mail, 1849-1869*. 1926. Reprint, New York: AMS Press, 1969.

Haines, Aubrey L. *Historic Sites along the Oregon Trail*. Gerald, Mo.: Patrice Press, 1981.

Henderson, Paul. "The Story of Mud Springs." *Nebraska History* 32, no. 2. (June 1951).

Howard, Robert West, Ray E. Coy, Frank C. Robertson, and Agnes Wright Spring. *Hoofbeats of Destiny: The Story of the Pony Express*. New York: Signet Books, New American Library of World Literature, 1960.

Inman, Col. Henry, and William F. Cody. *The Great Salt Lake Trail.* 1898. Reprint, Williamstown, Mass.: Corner House Pub., 1978.

Lewin, Jacqueline. "The Pony Express Trail in Kansas." *The Happenings* 18, no. 4 (1991).

Loving, Mabel. *The Pony Express Rides On.* St. Joseph, Mo.: Robidoux Printing Co., 1960.

Majors, Alexander. *Seventy Years on the Frontier.* 1893. Reprint. Minneapolis: Ross & Haines, 1965.

Mason, Dorothy. *The Pony Express in Nevada.* Comp. Nevada Bureau of Land Management. Reno: Harrah's, 1976.

Mattes, Merrill J., and Paul Henderson. *The Pony Express from St. Joseph to Fort Laramie.* Tucson: Patrice Press, 1989.

Mechem, Kirke, ed. "The Pony Express Rides Again." *Kansas Historical Quarterly* 25, no. 4 (Winter 1959).

Moeller, Bill, and Jan Moeller. *Crazy Horse: A Photographic Biography.* Missoula, Mont.: Mountain Press, 2000.

Moody, Ralph. *Riders of the Pony Express.* Boston: Houghton Mifflin, 1958.

Nebraska Game and Parks Commission. "The Oregon Trail." *Pamphlet,* n.d.

——. "Rock Creek Station." *Pamphlet,* n.d.

Reinfeld, Fred. *Pony Express.* Lincoln: University of Nebraska Press, 1966.

Settle, Raymond W., and Mary Lund Settle. *Saddles and Spurs: The Pony Express Saga.* Lincoln: University of Nebraska Press, 1955.

Smith, Waddell F. *The Story of the Pony Express.* San Francisco: Hesperian House Book Pub., 1960.

Townley, John M. *The Pony Express Guidebook: Across Nevada with the Pony Express and Overland Stage Line.* Reno: Great Basin Studies Center [1986].

Twain, Mark. *Roughing It.* 1872. Reprint. New York: Penguin Books, 1980.

Visscher, William Lightfoot. *The Pony Express: Blazing the Westward Way.* 1908. Reprint. Chicago: Charles T. Powner Co., 1946.

Wetmore, Helen Cody. *Last of the Great Scouts.* c. 1899. Reprint. New York: Tom Doherty Associates, 1996.

❋ INDEX ❋

❈ ABOUT THE AUTHORS ❈

Husband and wife **Bill** and **Jan Moeller** are professional photographers and authors. Since 1982 they have traveled full-time in their RV to photograph historical sites around the United States. Having their home with them allows the Moellers to stay in an area as long as necessary to take pictures and do research for their unique photographic history books.

Before embarking on their land-based ventures, the Moellers lived aboard a sailboat for twelve years, touring the Atlantic Coast. In addition to their photo histories, the authors have published books and articles on sailing and RVing. Other Moeller photographic history books published by Mountain Press include *Chief Joseph and the Nez Perces: A Photographic History* (ISBN 0-87842-319-2), *Lewis & Clark: A Photographic Journey* (ISBN 0-87842-405-9), and *Crazy Horse: A Photographic Biography* (ISBN 0-87842-424-5), and *The Oregon Trail: A Photographic Journey* (ISBN 0-87842-442-3).

OTHER BOOKS BY BILL AND JAN MOELLER:

The Oregon Trail: A Photographic Journey

Crazy Horse: A Photographic Biography

Lewis & Clark: A Photographic Journey

Chief Joseph and the Nez Perces:
A Photographic History

Custer, His Life, His Adventures:
A Photographic Biography

RVing Alaska by Land and Sea

A Complete Guide to Full-time RVing:
Life on the Open Road

RVing Basics

RV Electrical Systems

The Intracoastal Waterway:
A Cockpit Cruising Handbook

Living Aboard:
The Cruising Sailboat as a Home

We encourage you to patronize your local bookstore. Most stores will order any title that they do not stock. You may also order directly from Mountain Press using the order form provided below or by calling our toll-free number and using your credit card. We will gladly send you a complete catalog upon request.

Some other titles of interest:

_____Chief Joseph and the Nez Perces: *A Photographic History*	$15.00/paper	
_____The Oregon Trail: *A Photographic Journey*	$18.00/paper	
_____Crazy Horse: *A Photographic Biography*	$20.00/paper	
_____Lewis & Clark: *A Photographic Journey*	$18.00/paper	
_____The Pony Express: *A Photographic History*	$22.00/paper	
_____Sacagawea's Son: *The Life of Jean Baptiste Charbonneau*	$10.00/paper	
(for readers 10 and up)		
_____Stories of Young Pioneers: *In Their Own Words*	$14.00/paper	
(for readers 10 and up)		
_____The Arikara War: *The First Plains Indian War, 1823*	$18.00/paper	$30.00/cloth
_____The Journals of Patrick Gass:		
Member of the Lewis and Clark Expedition	$20.00/paper	
_____The Bloody Bozeman: *The Perilous Trail to Montana's Gold*	$16.00/paper	
_____Lakota Noon: *The Indian Narrative of Custer's Defeat*	$18.00/paper	$36.00/cloth
_____The Mystery of E Troop: *Custer's Gray Horse*		
Company at the Little Bighorn	$18.00/paper	
_____Children of the Fur Trade:		
Forgotten Métis of the Pacific Northwest	$15.00/paper	
_____The Piikani Blackfeet: *A Culture Under Siege*	$18.00/paper	$30.00/cloth
_____William Henry Jackson: *Framing the Frontier*	$22.00/paper	$36.00/cloth
_____The Saga of the Pony Express	$17.00/paper	$29.00/cloth

Please include $3.00 for 1-4 books or $5.00 for 5 or more books for shipping and handling.

Send the books marked above. I enclose $ _____

Name_____

Address_____

City/State/Zip_____

☐ Payment enclosed (check or money order in U.S. funds)

Bill my: ☐ VISA ☐ MasterCard ☐ American Express ☐ Discover   Exp. Date:_____

Card No._____

Signature_____

MOUNTAIN PRESS PUBLISHING COMPANY
P.O. Box 2399 • Missoula, MT 59806 • fax: 406-728-1635
Order Toll Free 1-800-234-5308 • Have your credit card ready.
e-mail: info@mtnpress.com • website: www.mountain-press.com